TIMELINE HISTORY

CLOTHES

From Furs to Fair Trade

Liz Miles

⒭ **www.raintreepublishers.co.uk**
Visit our website to find out more information about Raintree books.

To order:
☎ Phone 0845 6044371
🖹 Fax +44 (0) 1865 312263
🖥 Email myorders@raintreepublishers.co.uk

Customers from outside the UK please telephone +44 1865 312262

Raintree is an imprint of Capstone Global Library Limited, a company incorporated in England and Wales having its registered office at 7 Pilgrim Street, London, EC4V 6LB – Registered company number: 6695582

Edited by Louise Galpine and Diyan Leake
Designed by Richard Parker
Original illustrations © Capstone Global Library 2011
Illustrated by Jeff Edwards
Picture research by Hannah Taylor
Originated by Dot Gradations Ltd
Printed and bound in China by CTPS

ISBN 978 0 431 02552 0 (hardback)
14 13 12 11 10
10 9 8 7 6 5 4 3 2 1

British Library Cataloguing in Publication Data
Miles, Liz – Clothes : from furs to fair trade. – (Timeline history)
391'.009-dc22
A full catalogue record for this book is available from the British Library.

Acknowledgements
We would like to thank the following for permission to reproduce photographs: Alamy Images pp. **8** bottom (© Ivy Close Images), **25** (© Jon Arnold Images Ltd); Corbis pp. **4** bottom (Reed Kaestner), **7** bottom (Gianni Dagli Orti), **8** top (Werner Forman), **9** (Bettmann), **11** top (Charles & Josette Lenars), **13** bottom (Michael Maslan Historic Photographs), **13** top (Lebrecht Music & Arts), **18** top (Luca I. Tettoni), **18** bottom, **20** (Philip Gendreau), **21** bottom (Bettmann), **26** (Reuters/Jason Reed); Getty Images pp. **4** top (AFP Photo/Adrian Dennis), **6** (De Agostini Picture Library), **11** bottom (Arabian Eye), **23** bottom (Popperfoto), **27** (Simon Rawles); Photolibrary pp. **17** bottom (Art Media), **23** top (Jim Zuckerman); Rex Features pp. **7** top (Suedtirolfoto/Helmuth Rier), **10** (KPA/Zuma), **12** (Sipa Press), **19** (Everett Collection/ CSU Archives), **24** top (Jonathan Player), **24** bottom (Stills Press Agency); The Advertising Archives p. **21** top; The Art Archive pp. **14** top (Palazzo Pitti Florence/Dagli Orti), **14** bottom (Victoria & Albert Museum/Sally Chappell), **16** (Bibliothèque des Arts Décoratifs Paris/Dagli Orti), **17** top (Musée du Château de Versailles/Dagli Orti); TopFoto pp. **15**, **22**.

Cover photograph reproduced with permission of Getty Images (Iconica/Peter Cade).

We would like to thank Audrean Been for her invaluable help in the preparation of this book.

Contents

Historical time is divided into two major periods. BC is short for "before Christ" – that is, the time before the Christian religion began. This is the time up to the year 1 BC. AD is short for "Anno Domini". This is Latin for "in the year of our Lord", meaning the time from the year 1 BC to the present. For example, when a date is given as AD 1000, it is 1000 years after the year 1 BC. The abbreviation c. stands for *circa*, which is Latin for "around".

Any words appearing in the text in bold, **like this**, are explained in the glossary.

Why do people wear clothes?

Throughout history, people have worn clothes to survive. Clothes keep the body warm and protect it from the burning Sun. Clothes are worn for particular jobs, or as a uniform. Since the first **civilizations**, people have also worn clothes to gain admiration, or to show off. Clothes have long been used to show a person's status, **culture**, or religion.

Athletes wear clothes that help them excel at their sport.

Changing fashions

This book looks at how clothes have changed over time, and how they vary around the world according to taste, culture, climate, and wealth. Clothes also change in style as new materials, new processes, inventions, and new fashions take hold.

The evidence

Most ancient clothes rotted away long ago but **archaeologists** sometimes find rare fragments that have been preserved in dry or frozen climates. We can also find out what people wore in the past by looking at ancient art, such as paintings, pottery decorations, or carvings. Written descriptions are another useful source.

Ancient Egyptian pharaohs (kings) and queens wore **elaborate** costumes to show their god-like importance.

Timelines

The information in this book is on a timeline. A timeline shows you events from history in the order they happened. The big timeline in the middle of each page gives you details of a certain time in history (see below).

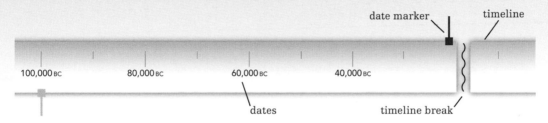

Some dates are exact. For example, the Singer sewing machine was invented in 1851. Others are more general because there were no written records about an event, or it took place over a period of time. The smaller timeline at the bottom of each page shows you how the page you are reading fits into history as a whole. You will read about clothes from all around the world. Each entry on the main timeline is in a different colour. This colour shows you which continent the information is about. The map below shows you how this colour coding works. Pale green indicates an event that took place on more than one continent or worldwide.

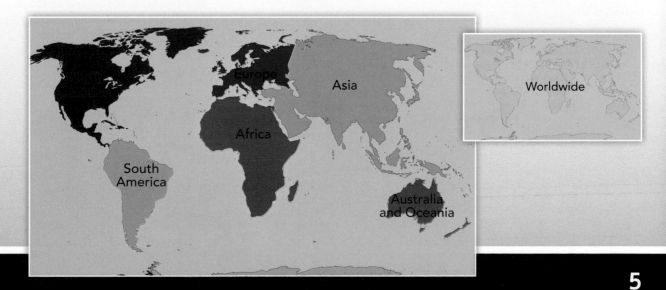

From skins to skirts

No one knows if the first humans wore clothes 200,000 years ago. They lived in warm parts of Africa. When they moved to cooler lands in Europe and Asia, animal-skin clothing might have kept them warm. Later, people made clothes from other natural **resources** such as plants and sheep wool.

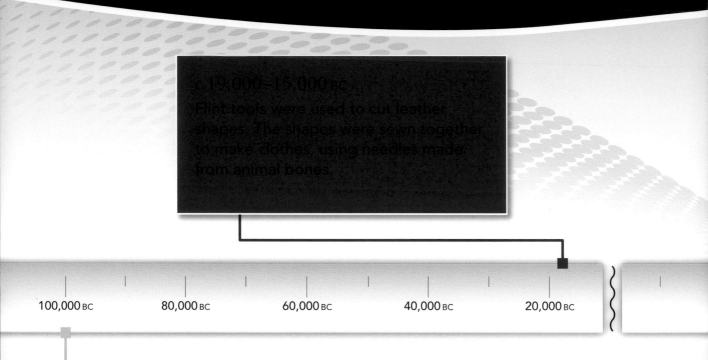

*c.*19,000–15,000 BC
Flint tools were used to cut leather shapes. The shapes were sewn together to make clothes, using needles made from animal bones.

100,000 BC	80,000 BC	60,000 BC	40,000 BC	20,000 BC

*c.*100,000–40,000 BC
Prehistoric people living in cold climates hunted for food and for animal furs and skins to keep themselves warm.

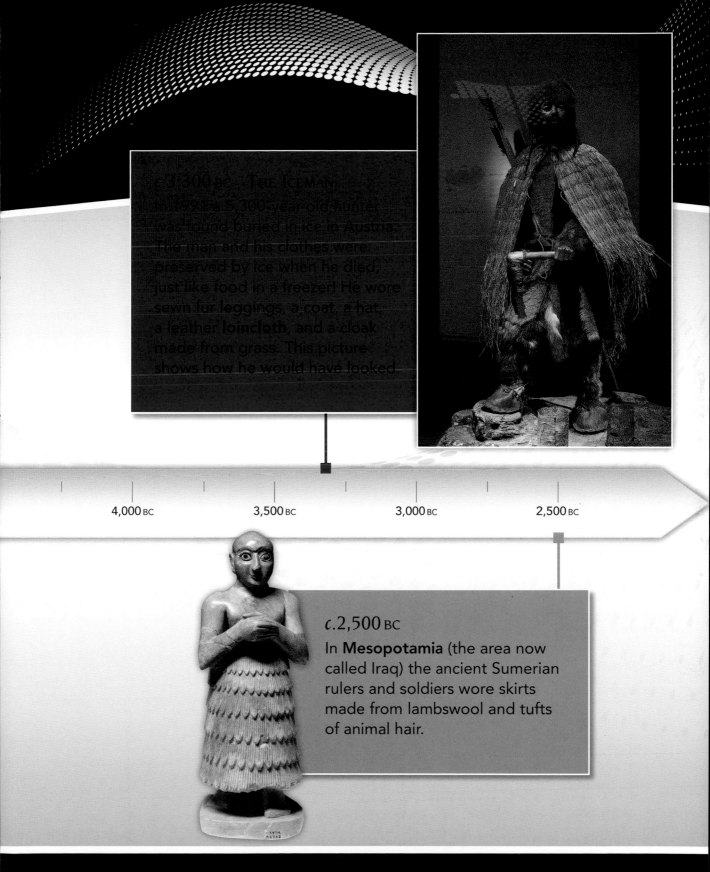

c.3,300 BC   THE ICEMAN
In 1991 a 5,300-year-old hunter
was found buried in ice in Austria.
The man and his clothes were
preserved by ice when he died,
just like food in a freezer! He wore
sewn fur leggings, a coat, a hat,
a leather loincloth, and a cloak
made from grass. This picture
shows how he would have looked.

4,000 BC   3,500 BC   3,000 BC   2,500 BC

*c.*2,500 BC

In **Mesopotamia** (the area now
called Iraq) the ancient Sumerian
rulers and soldiers wore skirts
made from lambswool and tufts
of animal hair.

Rich and poor

Ancient **civilizations** often used clothes to show people's rank, wealth, or power. Men and women wore different styles. **Elaborate** costumes were used for rituals and ceremonies, too. Materials for these costumes were dyed or decorated with stitching such as **embroidery**.

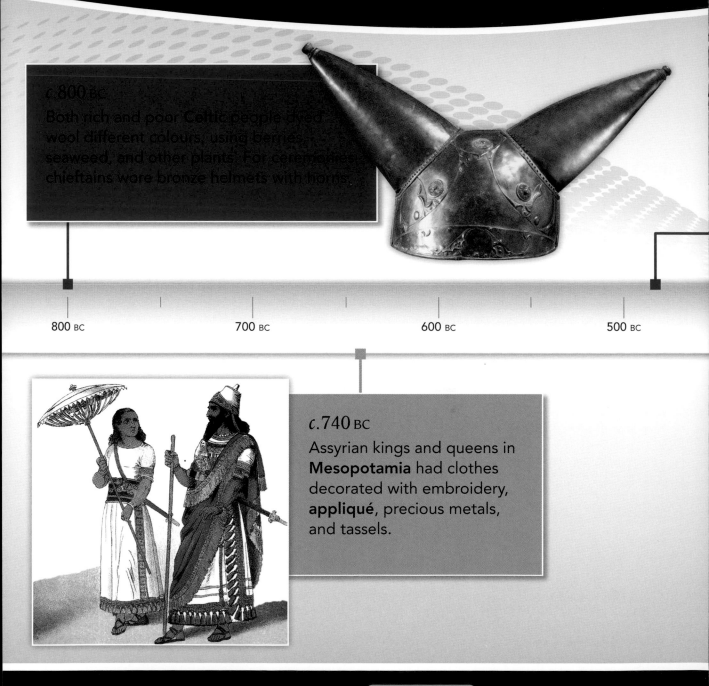

*c.*800 BC
Both rich and poor **Celtic** people dyed wool different colours, using berries, seaweed, and other plants. For ceremonies, chieftains wore bronze helmets with horns.

800 BC	700 BC	600 BC	500 BC

*c.*740 BC
Assyrian kings and queens in **Mesopotamia** had clothes decorated with embroidery, **appliqué**, precious metals, and tassels.

c.479 BC   Long for women, short for men

In ancient Greece, only the rich wore brightly coloured clothes. A law stopped poorer Athenians from wearing clothes dyed a reddish colour. A tunic called a peplos was popular. It was pinned at the shoulders. Men and women also wore a length of linen fabric called a chiton. Women wore their chitons long, but men wore them short.

400 BC   300 BC   200 BC

c.300 BC

In Peru one of the oldest forms of knitting was used to make hats and shawls. It was called needle-binding and it used one flat needle and lots of short pieces of yarn.

Magnificent materials

Trade brought a wider variety of clothing materials. The Roman Empire (in and around Europe) received silk and jewels from the East (China, Persia, and India). From 114 BC there was a trade route (the Silk Route) that brought many goods from China.

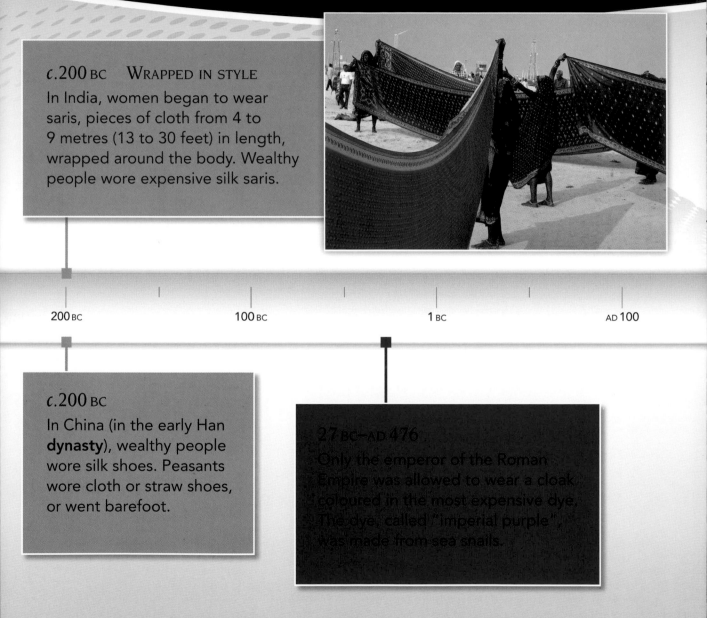

c.200 BC WRAPPED IN STYLE

In India, women began to wear saris, pieces of cloth from 4 to 9 metres (13 to 30 feet) in length, wrapped around the body. Wealthy people wore expensive silk saris.

200 BC	100 BC	1 BC	AD 100

c.200 BC

In China (in the early Han **dynasty**), wealthy people wore silk shoes. Peasants wore cloth or straw shoes, or went barefoot.

27 BC–AD 476

Only the emperor of the Roman Empire was allowed to wear a cloak coloured in the most expensive dye. The dye, called "imperial purple", was made from sea snails.

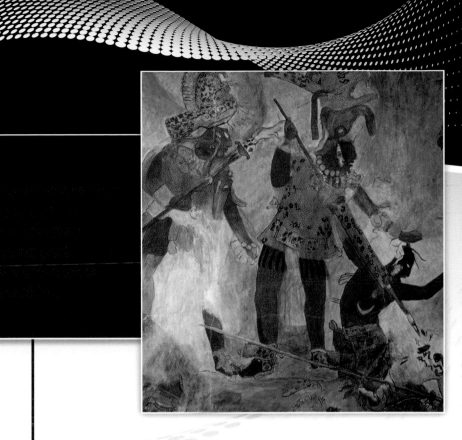

AD 200   AD 300   AD 400   AD 500

AD 300–500

Travelling Arab traders brought new styles of clothing to North Africa. Similar styles are still worn today. Their loose fit keeps the body cool while protecting it from the Sun.

Painful fashions

Most ordinary people wore practical clothes. Warm clothes were made from the skins or fur of animals, ranging from camels to seals. Clothes that were fashionable were not always very comfortable. Some clothes were painful to wear.

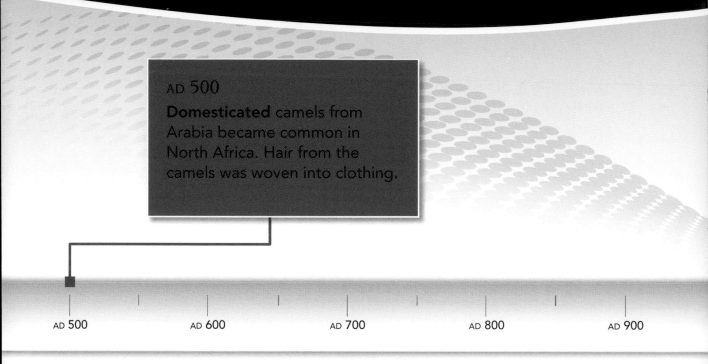

AD 500

Domesticated camels from Arabia became common in North Africa. Hair from the camels was woven into clothing.

AD 500   AD 600   AD 700   AD 800   AD 900

1100s

Girls in China (during the Song **dynasty**) had their feet bound from the age of about 5 years. It was painful and made them lame. It was thought that beautiful women had tiny feet. This practice went on into the 1900s.

1100s–1300s
MEDIEVAL EXTREMES

In Western Europe, very long pointed shoes were popular. The points were sometimes stiffened to curl upwards. Women wore very high hats called steeple hats. They plucked any hair that showed outside the hats. Medieval knights wore uncomfortable metal-plated armour. Some armour was so heavy that the knight had to be winched up on to his horse.

1000   1100   1200   1300   1400

Materials from afar

More trade routes were set up between Europe and the East. Fabrics were transported around the world. For example, beautiful Indian **chintzes** became popular in Europe. While **settlers** brought new clothing materials to other continents, invaders stole fabrics and jewels and took them home.

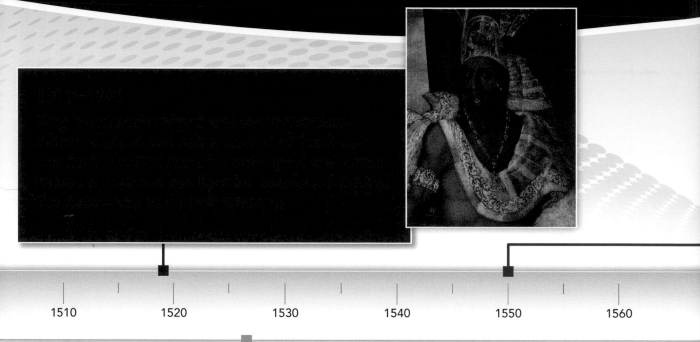

1510   1520   1530   1540   1550   1560

1526

In the Mughal Empire (1526–1857) in India, emperors wore a long-sleeved garment with long silk or cotton trousers called the *pyjama*. The same word is used in English today for some nightwear.

Mid-1500s STIFF AND STARCHY

A hooped underskirt called a farthingale was first worn by women in Spain. It forced the skirt out into the shape of a wheel or bell. The fashion spread to Germany, then England. Throughout Europe an ornate collar called a ruff became fashionable, too. **Starch** was used to make ruffs stick out as much as 20 centimetres (8 inches) from the neck.

1570   1580   1590   1600   1610

c.1610

No one knows when the first **kilt** was worn but around this time men in the Scottish highlands wore **tartan** skirts.

Different worlds

European explorers met people living in remote places for the first time. They wrote about foreign **cultures** and styles of clothing. People influenced clothes or fashions as they travelled around the world. The French royal court set the fashion in Europe.

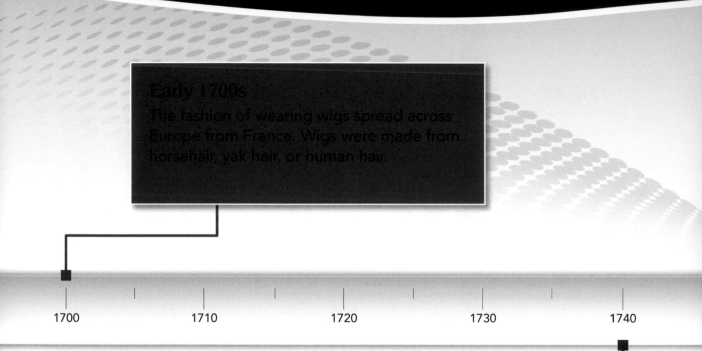

Early 1700s

The fashion of wearing wigs spread across Europe from France. Wigs were made from horsehair, yak hair, or human hair.

| 1700 | 1710 | 1720 | 1730 | 1740 |

1770s — Beneath the makeup
The French court was like an extreme fashion show. Women wore very wide skirts. Elaborate hairstyles were topped with amazing decorations. Powdered white wigs and powdered white faces were fashionable in Europe. Washing was seen as unhealthy. Thick make-up and painted beauty spots hid bad skin. Wigs became so dirty that lice, fleas, or even mice lived in them!

1778
The British explorer Captain Cook and his crew were the first Europeans to go to Hawaii. Hawaiians were dressed in **loincloths**, feather capes, and masks made from **gourds**.

1750	1760	1770	1780

Clothes for everyone

During the Industrial Revolution (1750–1850) in Europe, textile factories opened and new machinery was invented, such as the first powered **loom**. By the 1800s, **mass manufacturing** made it quicker and easier to make textiles.

1800s

In Thailand, headdresses worn by dancers (right) were made from a cheap metal. Those worn by royalty were made from gold.

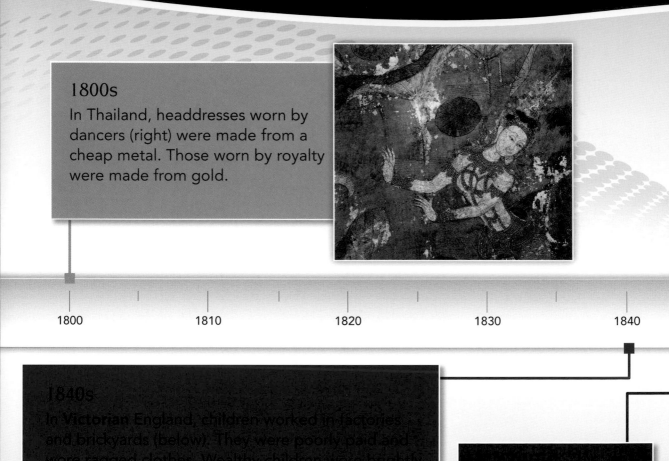

1800   1810   1820   1830   1840

1840s

In **Victorian** England, children worked in factories and brickyards (below). They were poorly paid and wore ragged clothes. Wealthy children wore brightly coloured clothes with pleats, buttons, and bows.

1870s
Englishman Charles Frederick Worth was one of the first dressmakers to design a seasonal collection of made-to-measure clothing.

Changing clothes

In Europe, World War I (1914–1918) influenced the way people dressed. Work clothes became more practical. Clothes were changing in other parts of the world, too, because of new ideas and inventions. European **colonial** powers influenced the clothes in the countries they ruled.

1900s

In Indonesia, white clothes had always been worn as a sign of grief when someone died. European colonial rulers there wore white as an everyday colour. Indonesians, like the workers here shown lifting mail sacks, soon did the same.

1900   1902   1904   1906   1908   1910

1914

By the start of World War I, army service uniforms had changed from bright colours to the shade of brown called khaki. Khaki was harder for the enemy to spot. **Camouflage** patterns came a year later.

THE SATURDAY EVENING POST

Put Your Family in

Keds

Canvas Rubber-soled Footwear for Men, Women and Children

KEDS is the name to guide you to grace, beauty and solid comfort in footwear. Keds is the new name of an old-established family of ultra-stylish, serviceable and comfortable rubber-soled shoes with uppers of a specially woven fine grade of canvas.

If you glory in a light, springy step, full of noiseless grace, ask your dealer for Keds. There are many styles and shapes. You can find your particular Keds, whether for the fashionable boulevard or afternoon tea on your own porch.

Keds are vogue—they are worn by particular dressers at all the smart places—they add a refreshing grace to the dainty feet of society women—they give substantial wear with good looks and solid comfort to business men—for children they are next to going "barefoot."

There are three grades of Keds. Choose the kind you want. You are sure of wear in every pair. Each grade carries with it the reputation of the largest rubber manufacturer in the world.

$1.50 up

$1.25 to $2.00

$1.00 to $1.50

NATIONAL Keds

CAMPFIRE Keds

Keds

There is style in Keds. They are built on popular lasts and approved by fashion authorities.

There is comfort in Keds. The tops offer full, elastic support; the soles are durable, flexible and buoyant.

There is economy in Keds. Cost considered, Keds outwear any other footwear yet devised.

Ask your dealer to show you Keds and shoe the family in style and comfort.

United States Rubber Company

New York

1912   1914   1916   1918   1920

1920s FLAPPERS

Women's fashion took on a boyish look. It included short hair, breast-flattening bras, and straight, short skirts. Young women in the 20s became known as "flappers". Free of stuffy **Victorian** ways, they danced to the jazz music of the day.

Setting new trends

Hollywood stars in the new movie industry began to set fashion trends in the 1930s. Money poured into the fashion industry as wealthy people bought increasingly showy clothes. Inventions led to new, ever-changing fashions.

1937
A newly designed zip inspired French fashion designers to swap buttons for zips on men's trousers. Children's clothes with zips were popular, too.

1946
The modern bikini was invented. It was advertised as "smaller than the smallest swimsuit".

1930   1935   1940   1945   1950

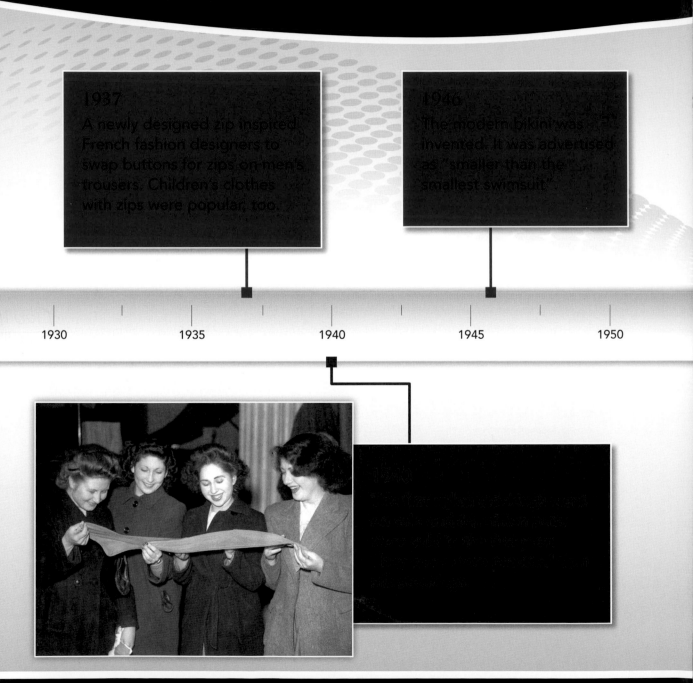

1963

As many African **colonies** became independent, semi-nude tribes were told to "cover up" in the name of "development". In 1963 the Tanzanian government tried to force the Masaai peoples (above) to give up their traditional clothes.

1966 SWINGING 60S

British designer Mary Quant and models such as Twiggy made the miniskirt popular. Later in the 1960s, casual hippy clothes became fashionable, with long skirts and flowery fabrics.

Self-expression

People began to use extreme clothes as a form of self-expression. Trouser fashions in the 1970s ranged from hotpants to bell-bottoms; shoes from hippy sandals to platforms. Styles at the **turn of the century** ranged from **goth** to **grunge**.

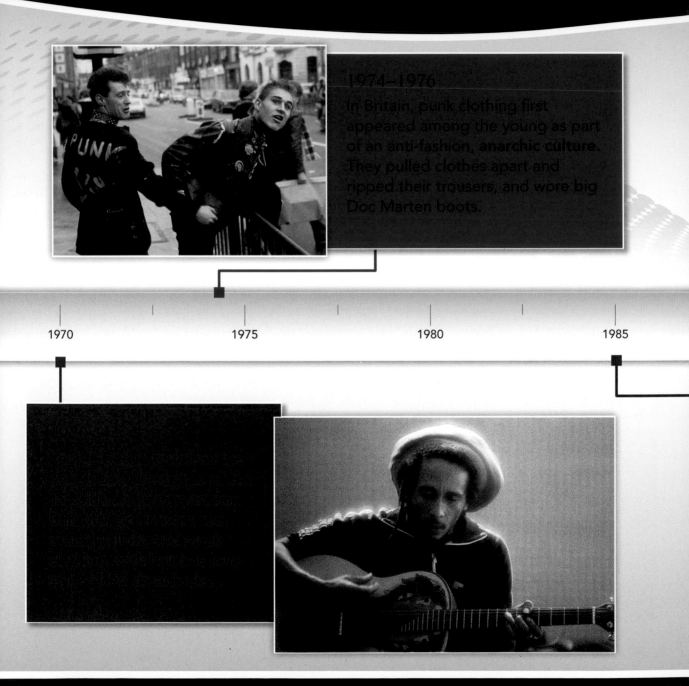

1974–1976
In Britain, punk clothing first appeared among the young as part of an anti-fashion, anarchic culture. They pulled clothes apart and ripped their trousers, and wore big Doc Marten boots.

1970   1975   1980   1985

Present

An extreme style called *kawaii* ("cuteness") has been the in-thing in Japan. Fashionable young teenagers wear artificial flowers, bows, and big buttons, or retro prints with punk-style skull-and-crossbones jewellery.

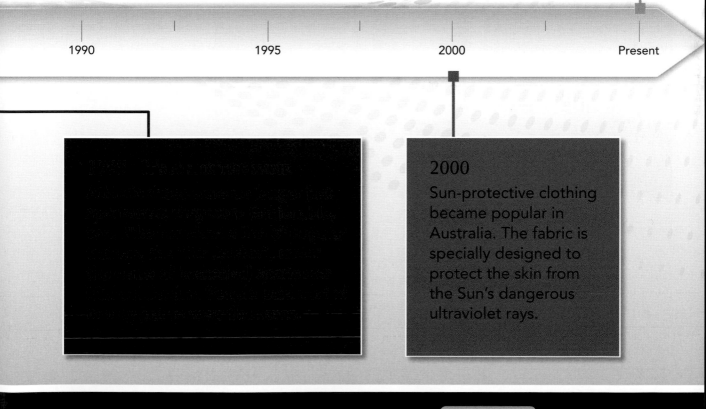

1990   1995   2000   Present

2000

Sun-protective clothing became popular in Australia. The fabric is specially designed to protect the skin from the Sun's dangerous ultraviolet rays.

Fashion and fair trade

Many people believe that fashion goes in cycles. Some parents see their children wearing clothes that they themselves wore decades ago. Vintage clothing, bought from second-hand or antique shops, has been a popular fashion since the early 2000s.

Some styles always look fashionable, like this evening wear worn by actor Evan Rachel Wood at an awards ceremony in 2009.

Exploitation

In the Western world, clothing that is easy to maintain (wash and iron), or clothes that are cheap enough to throw away after a short time, have become very popular. However, to be able to sell at cheap prices, some clothes companies exploit workers in poorer countries by not paying them a decent wage.

This fair trade farmer in Mali, Africa, gets a fair price for the cotton that she grows.

Fair trade

Fair trade organizations check that clothes and materials bought in developing countries are bought and sold for a fair price. Campaigns to buy clothes made in the buyer's own country say that this avoids taking advantage of poorer nations.

Sustainability

Concerns about the environment are also affecting the clothes industry. Cotton for some clothing is grown organically, so that there is less damage to the environment and wildlife.

Recycling clothes saves **resources**. Companies such as Patagonia make garments that can be returned and recycled once they are worn out. Companies also recycle household waste and make it into clothing materials. For example, used plastic bottles can be made into fabric to make fleece jackets.

New environmental challenges may inspire the fashion industry to come up with new ideas – and unique clothes.

Key dates

c.100,000–40,000 BC
Prehistoric people living in cold climates drape themselves in animal furs and skins.

c.2,500 BC
In **Mesopotamia** the ancient Sumerian rulers and soldiers wear skirts made from lambswool and tufts of animal hair.

c.800 BC
Celtic people dye wool different colours, using berries, seaweed, and other plants.

c.200 BC
Women begin to wear saris (long pieces of cloth wrapped around the body).

AD 300
In the Mayan **civilization** (in the areas we now know as Guatemala and Mexico), wealthy soldiers wear cloaks made from jaguar skins.

1100s
Girls in China (during the Song **dynasty**) have their feet bound from the age of about 5 years. It is thought that beautiful women have tiny feet.

1100s–1300s
Medieval knights wear uncomfortable metal-plated armour.

1519–1521
Spanish invaders steal gold and jewels used by the religious and ruling classes of the Aztec Empire in **Central America** to adorn their clothes.

Mid-1500s
A hooped underskirt called a farthingale is first worn by women in Spain.

c.1610
Men in the Scottish highlands wear **tartan** skirts.

1770s
Women in France wear very wide skirts and **elaborate** hairstyles topped with amazing decorations.

1778
Hawaiians dress in **loincloths**, feather capes, and **gourd** masks.

1851
The invention of Isaac Merritt Singer's sewing machines leads to the **mass manufacture** of clothing.

1870s
Charles Frederick Worth is one of the first dressmakers to design a seasonal collection of made-to-measure clothing.

1917
Keds, trainer-like shoes with canvas tops and rubber soles, become popular in the United States.

1920s
Women's fashion takes on a boyish look, including short hair, breast-flattening bras, and straight, short skirts.

1937
Buttons are swapped for zips on men's trousers and children's clothes.

1959
The factory-made fibre **spandex** is **patented**.

1970s–present
An extreme style called *kawaii* ("cuteness") becomes the fashion for young people in Japan.

2000
Clothing designed to protect the skin from the Sun's dangerous ultraviolet rays becomes popular in Australia.

Glossary

anarchic having no order, breaking rules

appliqué decoration on clothes. Appliqué involves sewing smaller pieces of material on to fabric.

archaeologist someone who studies the past by digging up and examining things people used to use

camouflage material coloured to match the land. Camouflage-patterned material is the colour of trees, soil, or sand.

Celtic people who lived in central Europe from around 800 BC

Central America the part of North America in between Mexico and South America

chintz boldly patterned material

civilization particular society or culture at a particular period of time

colonial having to do with colonies

colony area or country that is ruled by another country

culture customs and beliefs that a group of people have

domesticated trained to live with people

dynasty period of rule of a particular family

elaborate having complicated detail or decoration

embroidery design or pictures sewn on to material

feminist someone who believes that women should have the same rights as men

goth style of clothes and music which began in the United Kingdom in the 1980s. Black clothes and make-up are a part of goth fashion.

gourd dried shell of a hard-skinned fruit

grunge 1990s fashion that had an untidy look. Clothes for a grunge look were often bought in second-hand shops.

kilt skirt that men wear

loincloth piece of cloth that men wear, wrapped around the hips and between the legs

loom machine for weaving cloth

mass manufacturing making lots of the same items in a factory. A mass-manufactured item is usually cheaper than a hand-made version.

Mesopotamia the part of the world we now call Iraq, as well as some parts of Syria, Turkey, and Iran

nylon a strong fabric made from chemicals

patent record as an invention. Once its inventor has patented an item, no one else can make, use, or sell it for some time.

prehistoric before there was any form of writing

resource something that can be used

settler person who goes to live in a different land

sinew animal tissue that joins muscles to bones

spandex factory-made, strong but stretchable fabric. Lycra is a type of spandex.

starch substance used to whiten and stiffen clothes. Starch is found in foods such as potato and flour.

sustainability ability to last

tartan cloth with a plaid, or chequered, pattern

turn of the century time of transition from one century to another

Victorian the period in the United Kingdom when Queen Victoria reigned (1837–1901)

Find out more

Books

Clothes: Discover How People Dressed Around the World with 30 Great Step-by-step Projects **(Hands-On History Projects series)**, Rachel Halstead and Struan Reid (Southwater, 2008)

Would You Believe ... in 1500, Platform Shoes Were Outlawed?: and Other Fashion Follies, Richard Platt (Oxford University Press, 2008)

Websites

Lots of shoes at the Bata Shoe Museum site:
www.batashoemuseum.ca

For more information about textiles and clothing:
library.thinkquest.org/C004179

Places to visit

See the fashion and jewellery collection:
V&A Museum
South Kensington
Cromwell Road
London SW7 2RL
Tel. 0207 7942 2000
Email: vanda@vam.ac.uk

See the clothing collection:
Walsall Museum
Lichfield Street
Walsall
West Midlands WS1 1TR
Tel. 01922 653116
Email: museum@walsall.gov.uk

See the boot and shoe collection:
Northampton Museum and Art Gallery
Guildhall Road
Northampton NN1 1DP
Tel. 01604 838111
Email: museums@northampton.gov.uk

Index